Artists'
Birthday Book

Third Edition
Manufactured in China

Produced by the Department of Special Publications, The Metropolitan Museum of Art: Robie Rogge, Publishing Manager; Mimi Tribble, Assistant Editor; Anna Raff, Designer; Mahin Kooros, Production Associate.
All photography by The Metropolitan Museum of Art Photograph Studio.

Visit the Museum's Web site: www.metmuseum.org

Distributed in Canada by
Raincoast Books
9050 Shaughnessy Street
Vancouver, BC V6P 6E5

10 9 8 7 6 5 4 3 2 1

Chronicle Books LLC
680 Second Street
San Francisco, CA 94107
www.chroniclebooks.com

ISBN 0-87099-810-2 (MMA)
ISBN 0-8118-5849-9 (Chronicle Books)

Artists'
Birthday Book

CHRONICLE BOOKS
SAN FRANCISCO

THE METROPOLITAN MUSEUM OF ART • NEW YORK

Washington Crossing the Delaware
Emanuel Leutze, American, 1816–1868 (May 24)

Since 1977, The Metropolitan Museum of Art's *Birthday Book* has delighted, educated, and charmed many, and so in honor of its thirtieth anniversary, we have given it a makeover. While the look of this edition is different, the idea remains the same—it is a permanent calendar that lists the birthdays of more than 800 people connected to the arts, with ample room to write in the birthdays of family and friends.

For the first edition, a committee of curators determined those who are included, a selection that was updated in 1996 and again recently as contemporary artists, such as Cindy Sherman (January 19), Frank Gehry (February 28), and Jean-Michel Basquiat (December 22), have flourished. The artists represent the wide scope of the Museum's collection from painters to photographers to sculptors to designers to architects to musical-instrument makers to illustrators.

There are omissions—some from lack of information, others from lack of space. The birthdays of notable artists such as Hans Holbein, Titian, El Greco, and many non-Western artists, including Suzuki Kiitsu, whose work *Morning Glories* graces the cover, are still unknown. And because the format allows for three names only, some celebrated artists were dropped, albeit with reluctance, while lesser-known names are included because they do not share a birthday.

The biographical information that accompanies each name is how the artist is best known, which is not necessarily the name or nation of birth or the only medium an artist used. Count Balthazar Klossowski de Rola is better known as Balthus (February 29). Emanuel Leutze (May 24) was born in Germany but is decidedly American, reiterated by his well-known painting *Washington Crossing the Delaware.* The prolific Pablo Picasso (October 25) was a painter, sculptor, printmaker, designer, and draftsman; here he is described, for simplicity, as artist. Where space allowed, we tried to give as much information as possible. Edgar Degas (July 19) is noted as a painter, sculptor, and printmaker. A few of the birthdays are baptism dates, but we decided to use the available information anyway.

The works of art that illustrate this book include long-standing favorites, less familiar works that complement this edition's rejuvenation, and recent acquisitions that reflect the contemporized design. All are in the Museum's collection.

It is worth noting that the birthdays listed in this book tend to cluster; on certain days and weeks, the notable names stack up. Both Vincent van Gogh and Francisco de Goya were born on March 30, while Giovanni Battista Piranesi, Jean François Millet, and Frederic Remington were born on October 4. The week of July 5–12 is perhaps the most remarkable, with the birthdays of thirteen well-known artists: Chuck Close, Marc Chagall, Käthe Kollwitz, Philip Johnson, Minor White, David Hockney, Camille Pissarro, Giorgio de Chirico, James McNeill Whistler, Giorgio Armani, Josiah Wedgwood, Amedeo Modigliani, and Andrew Wyeth. Yet for other days and weeks, the pickings are slim; August 26 and 27 are conspicuously vacant.

We hope you enjoy this celebration of art and life, and Happy Birthday!

An Icy Night
Alfred Stieglitz, American, 1864–1946

1
Bartolomé Esteban Murillo, Spanish painter, 1618
Paul Revere, American silversmith, 1735
Alfred Stieglitz, American photographer, 1864

2
Ernst Barlach, German sculptor, 1870
Charles Howard, American painter, 1899
Robert Smithson, American sculptor, 1938

3
Augustin de Saint-Aubin, French printmaker, 1736
August Macke, German painter, 1887
Jack Levine, American painter, 1915

4
François Rude, French sculptor, 1784
Marsden Hartley, American painter, 1877
Wilhelm Lehmbruck, German sculptor, 1881

5
Bernard Leach, English ceramist, 1887
Yves Tanguy, American painter, 1900
Nicolas de Staël, French painter, 1914

6
Gustave Doré, French printmaker, 1832
Jean Ipoustéguy, French sculptor, 1920

January

7

Albert Bierstadt, American painter, 1830
P. A. J. Dagnan-Bouveret, French painter, 1852

8

Simon Vouet, French painter, 1590
Jacques-François Blondel, French architect, 1705
Sir Lawrence Alma-Tadema, English painter, 1836

9

Nicolas Coustou, French sculptor, 1658
William Powell Frith, English painter, 1819

10

John Wellborn Root, American architect, 1850
John Held, Jr., American illustrator, 1889
Barbara Hepworth, English sculptor, 1903

11

Parmigianino, Italian painter, 1503
Alexander Stirling Calder, American sculptor, 1870

12

John Singer Sargent, American painter, 1856

Two Girls on a Lawn
John Singer Sargent, American, 1856–1925

Still Life with Roses and Fruit
Henri Fantin-Latour, French, 1836–1904

13

Jan Josephsz. van Goyen, Dutch painter, 1596
Paul Gavarni, French printmaker, 1804

14

Henri Fantin-Latour, French painter, 1836
Berthe Morisot, French painter, 1841
Cecil Beaton, English photographer, 1904

15

Ferdinand Waldmüller, Austrian painter, 1793
Frances B. Johnston, American photographer, 1864
Andreas Gursky, German photographer, 1955

16

Samuel McIntire, American architect, 1757
Seymour Joseph Guy, American painter, 1824

17

Pieter van Bloemen, Flemish painter, 1657
Laurent Delvaux, Flemish sculptor, 1696

18

Antoine Pevsner, Russian sculptor, 1886
Philippe Starck, French architect, designer, 1949
Kiki Smith, American sculptor, printmaker, 1954

19
Paul Cézanne, French painter, 1839
Cindy Sherman, American artist, 1954

20
John Goddard, American cabinetmaker, 1723
Hippolyte Bayard, French photographer, 1801

21
Cristóbal Balenciaga, Spanish couturier, 1895
Christian Dior, French couturier, 1905
Jeff Koons, American conceptual artist, 1955

22
Nicolas Lancret, French painter, 1690
Francis Picabia, French painter, 1879
Guillermo Kuitca, Argentine painter, 1961

23
François Mansart, French architect, 1598
Édouard Manet, French painter, 1832
Georg Baselitz, German painter, printmaker, 1938

24
Gillis van Coninxloo, Flemish painter, 1544
Sir John Vanbrugh, English architect, 1664
Robert Motherwell, American painter, 1915

Apples
Paul Cézanne, French, 1839–1906

Merengue en Boca Chica
Rafael Ferrer, American (b. Puerto Rico), b. 1933

25
Pompeo Batoni, Italian painter, 1708
Rafael Ferrer, American painter, sculptor, 1933
Bill Viola, American video artist, 1951

26
Giovanni Lanfranco, Italian painter, 1582
Jean-Baptiste Pigalle, French sculptor, 1714
Kees van Dongen, French painter, 1877

27
Samuel Palmer, English painter, 1805
Lewis Carroll, English photographer, 1832
Eugène Carrière, French painter, 1849

28
John Baskerville, English printer, 1706
Jackson Pollock, American painter, 1912
Claes Oldenburg, American sculptor, 1929

29
William Sharp, English printmaker, 1749
Barnett Newman, American painter, 1905
Peter Voulkos, American sculptor, 1924

30
Balthasar Neumann, German architect, 1687
Bernardo Bellotto, Italian painter, 1721
Finn Juhl, Danish industrial designer, 1912

January–February

31

1
Thomas Cole, American painter, 1801
Mario Bellini, Italian designer, architect, 1935

2
Guercino, Italian painter, 1591
Sébastien Bourdon, French painter, 1616
George Loring Brown, American painter, 1814

3
J. J. Shannon, English painter, 1862
Norman Rockwell, American illustrator, 1894
Alvar Aalto, Finnish architect, 1898

4
Fernand Léger, French painter, 1881
Manuel Alvarez Bravo, Mexican photographer, 1902

5
Alison Saar, American sculptor, 1956

Three Women by a Garden
Fernand Léger, French, 1881–1955

The Tomb of Sir Walter Scott in Dryburgh Abbey
William Henry Fox Talbot, English, 1800–1877

6

Henry Fuseli, Swiss painter, 1741
Henry Hardenbergh, American architect, 1847
Othon Friesz, French painter, 1879

7

8

John Ruskin, English art critic, 1819
Franz Marc, German painter, 1880

9

J. J. P. Oud, Dutch architect, 1890
Robert Morris, American sculptor, 1931
Gerhard Richter, German painter, 1932

10

11

Nicolas-Antoine Taunay, French painter, 1755
W. H. F. Talbot, English photographer, 1800
Carlo Carrà, Italian painter, 1881

February

12
Thomas Moran, American painter, 1837
Eugène Atget, French photographer, 1857
Max Beckmann, German painter, 1884

13
Giovanni Battista Piazzetta, Italian painter, 1682
Philibert-Louis Debucourt, French painter, 1755
Grant Wood, American painter, 1892

14
Leon Battista Alberti, Italian architect, 1404

15
Henry Steinway, American piano maker, 1797
Charles-François Daubigny, French painter, 1817

16
Giovanni Battista Bodoni, Italian printer, 1740
Armand Guillaumin, French painter, 1841

17
Jusepe de Ribera, Spanish painter, 1591
John Townsend, American cabinetmaker, 1733
Raphaelle Peale, American painter, 1774

Still Life with Cake
Raphaelle Peale, American, 1774–1825

Victorian Interior II
Horace Pippin, American, 1888–1946

18

Michelangelo Cerquozzi, Italian painter, 1602
Louis Comfort Tiffany, American designer, 1848
Max Klinger, German painter, 1857

19

Jean-Baptiste Lemoyne, French sculptor, 1704
Constantin Brancusi, French sculptor, 1876
Lucio Fontana, Italian sculptor, 1899

20

Elie Nadelman, American sculptor, 1882
Louis I. Kahn, American architect, 1901
Ansel Adams, American photographer, 1902

21

H. P. Berlage, Dutch architect, 1856
Hubert de Givenchy, French couturier, 1927
Sue Coe, English artist, 1951

22

Charles-Nicolas Cochin II, French printmaker, 1715
Rembrandt Peale, American painter, 1778
Horace Pippin, American painter, 1888

23

Sir William Chambers, English architect, 1723
George Frederick Watts, English painter, 1817
Tom Wesselmann, American painter, 1931

February

24
Mattia Preti, Italian painter, 1613
Charles Le Brun, French painter, 1619
Winslow Homer, American painter, 1836

25
Jacques-Philippe Caresme, French painter, 1734
Pierre-Auguste Renoir, French painter, 1841
Heinrich Kühn, German photographer, 1866

26
Honoré Daumier, French painter, printmaker, 1808
Elihu Vedder, American painter, 1836
Kazimir Malevich, Russian painter, 1878

27
Joaquin Sorolla y Bastida, Spanish painter, 1863
Marino Marini, Italian sculptor, 1901

28
Sir John Tenniel, English illustrator, 1820
Frank Gehry, American architect, designer, 1929

29
Balthus, French painter, 1908

A Wall, Nassau
Winslow Homer, American, 1836–1910

Studies for the Libyan Sibyl
Michelangelo Buonarroti, Italian (Florentine), 1475–1564

1

A. W. N. Pugin, English architect, 1812
Augustus Saint-Gaudens, American sculptor, 1848
Oskar Kokoschka, Austrian painter, 1886

2

Albert Herter, American tapestry designer, 1871

3

Arnold Newman, American photographer, 1918

4

Sir Henry Raeburn, Scottish painter, 1756

5

Giovanni Battista Tiepolo, Italian painter, 1696
James Merritt Ives, American lithographer, 1824
Howard Pyle, American illusrator, 1853

6

Michelangelo Buonarroti, Italian artist, 1475

March

7
Sir Edwin Landseer, English painter, 1802
Piet Mondrian, Dutch painter, 1872
Milton Avery, American painter, 1885

8
Rosso Fiorentino, Italian painter, 1494
Anselm Kiefer, German painter, printmaker, 1945

9
David Smith, American sculptor, 1906
André Courrèges, French couturier, 1923

10
Domingos de Sequeira, Portuguese painter, 1768
William Etty, English painter, 1787

11
Charles Lock Eastlake, English architect, 1836
Kenneth Hayes Miller, American painter, 1876

12
Anton Raphael Mengs, German painter, 1728
David d'Angers, French sculptor, 1788
Anish Kapoor, Indian sculptor, 1954

The Steeplechase, Coney Island
Milton Avery, American, 1885–1965

The Green Car
William Glackens, American, 1870–1938

13
Johann Zoffany, English painter, 1733
Karl Fredrich Schinkel, German architect, 1781
William Glackens, American painter, 1870

14
Georges de La Tour, French painter, 1593
Reginald Marsh, American painter, 1898
Diane Arbus, American photographer, 1923

15

16
Juan Martínez Montañés, Spanish sculptor, 1568
Baron Antoine-Jean Gros, French painter, 1771
Rosa Bonheur, French painter, 1822

17
Jean-Baptiste Oudry, French painter, 1686
Kate Greenaway, English illustrator, 1846

18
Adam Elsheimer, German painter, 1578

March

19
Albert Pinkham Ryder, American painter, 1847
Josef Albers, American painter, 1888

20
George Caleb Bingham, American painter, 1811

21
Claude-Nicolas Ledoux, French architect, 1736
Hans Hofmann, American painter, 1880
Eric Mendelsohn, American architect, 1887

22
Anthony van Dyck, Flemish painter, 1599
Thomas Crawford, American sculptor, 1813
John Frederick Kensett, American painter, 1816

23
Joseph Christian Leyendecker, American illustrator, 1874
Juan Gris, Spanish painter, 1887
Francesco Clemente, Italian painter, 1952

24
John Smibert, American painter, 1688
William Morris, English designer, 1834
Edward Weston, American photographer, 1886

Still Life with a Guitar
Juan Gris, Spanish, 1887–1927

Oleanders
Vincent van Gogh, Dutch, 1853–1890

25
Jean-Antoine Houdon, French sculptor, 1741
Jack Youngerman, American painter, 1926
Matthew Barney, American artist, 1967

26
Hubert-François Gravelot, French illustrator, 1699
Alexej von Jawlensky, German painter, 1864
Shirin Neshat, Iranian photographer, 1957

27
Edward Steichen, American photographer, 1879
Ludwig Mies van der Rohe, German architect, 1886

28
Fra Bartolommeo, Italian painter, 1472
Grace Hartigan, American painter, 1922
Anthony Caro, English sculptor, 1924

29
Sir Edwin Landseer Lutyens, English architect, 1869

30
Francisco de Goya, Spanish painter, 1746
Vincent van Gogh, Dutch painter, 1853
Koloman Moser, Austrian designer, 1868

31
William Morris Hunt, American painter, 1824
John La Farge, American painter, 1835

1
Edwin Austin Abbey, American painter, 1852
Dan Flavin, American sculptor, 1933
Mario Botta, Swiss architect, 1943

2
William Holman Hunt, English painter, 1827
Frédéric-Auguste Bartholdi, French sculptor, 1834
Max Ernst, German painter, 1891

3
Henry van de Velde, Belgian architect, 1863
Russel Wright, American designer, 1904

4
Grinling Gibbons, English wood-carver, 1648
Jean Honoré Fragonard, French painter, 1732
Pierre-Paul Prud'hon, French painter, 1758

5
Jules Dupré, French painter, 1811

Portrait of a Woman with a Dog
Jean Honoré Fragonard, French, 1732–1806

Mirror Lake—Valley of the Yosemite
Eadweard Muybridge, American (b. England), 1830–1904

6
Raphael, Italian painter, 1483
Gustave Moreau, French painter, 1826
René Lalique, French jeweler, glassmaker, 1860

7
Gerard Dou, Dutch painter, 1613
Gino Severini, Italian painter, 1883
John B. Flannagan, American sculptor, 1895

8
Nadar, French photographer, 1820
Clarence H. White, American photographer, 1871
Richard Neutra, American architect, 1892

9
Eadweard Muybridge, American photographer, 1830
Charles Burchfield, American painter, 1893
Victor Vasarely, French painter, 1908

10
Ben Nicholson, English painter, 1894
Kenneth Noland, American painter, 1924

11
Gustav Vigeland, Norwegian sculptor, 1869

April

12
François-Joseph Bélanger, French architect, 1744
Imogen Cunningham, American photographer, 1883
Robert Delaunay, French painter, 1885

13
Thomas Jefferson, American architect, 1743
Sir Thomas Lawrence, English painter, 1769
James Ensor, Belgian painter, 1860

14
Gabriel de Saint-Aubin, French printmaker, 1724

15
Leonardo da Vinci, Italian painter, 1452
Charles Willson Peale, American painter, 1741
Arshile Gorky, American painter, 1904

16
Jules Hardouin Mansart, French architect, 1646
Elisabeth Louise Vigée Le Brun, French painter, 1755
John Chamberlain, American sculptor, 1927

17

A Bear Walking
Leonardo da Vinci, Italian (Florentine), 1452–1519

Animated Landscape
Joan Miró, Spanish, 1893–1983

18
Max Weber, American painter, 1881
Ludwig Meidner, German painter, 1884
Wynn Bullock, American photographer, 1902

19
Ludovico Carracci, Italian painter, 1555
William Klein, American photographer, 1928
Fernando Botero, Colombian sculptor, painter, 1932

20
Odilon Redon, French painter, printmaker, 1840
Joan Miró, Spanish painter, 1893
April Gornik, American painter, 1953

21
Humphry Repton, English landscape architect, 1752
Jean Hélion, French painter, 1904

22
Sidney Nolan, Australian painter, 1917
Richard Diebenkorn, American painter, 1922

23
Joseph M. W. Turner, English painter, 1775
Halston, American fashion designer, 1932

April

24
John Russell Pope, American architect, 1873
Willem de Kooning, American painter, 1904

25
Giovanni Battista Foggini, Italian sculptor, 1652
Georg Raphael Donner, Austrian sculptor, 1693
Cy Twombly, American painter, 1928

26
Eugène Delacroix, French painter, 1798
Frederick Law Olmsted, American landscape architect, 1822

27
Samuel F. B. Morse, American painter, 1791
Norman Bel Geddes, American stage designer, 1893

28
Yves Klein, French painter, 1928
Nancy Grossman, American painter, sculptor, 1940
William Kentridge, South African artist, 1955

29
David Hoadley, American architect, 1774
David Cox, English painter, 1783

Basket of Flowers
Eugène Delacroix, French, 1798–1863

Autumn Oaks
George Inness, American, 1825–1894

30
Jean-Jacques Caffiéri, French sculptor, 1725

1
George Inness, American painter, 1825
Jules Breton, French painter, 1827
Cecilia Beaux, American painter, 1855

2
Peggy Bacon, American printmaker, 1895

3
Alexandre-Gabriel Decamps, French painter, 1803
Jacob Riis, American photographer, 1849
Richard Lippold, American sculptor, 1915

4
Bartolomeo Cristofori, Italian piano maker, 1655
Frederic Edwin Church, American painter, 1826
Émile Gallé, French glassmaker, 1846

5
Donald Sultan, American artist, 1951

6

Ernst Ludwig Kirchner, German painter, 1880
Carlo Mollino, Italian designer, 1905

7

Richard Norman Shaw, English architect, 1831

8

Alphonse Legros, French painter, 1837

9

François Pompon, French sculptor, 1855
Gordon Bunschaft, American architect, 1909
Gary Hume, English painter, 1962

10

Léon Bakst, Russian stage designer, 1866

11

Alfred Stevens, Belgian painter, 1823
Jean-Baptiste Carpeaux, French sculptor, 1827
Salvador Dali, Spanish painter, printmaker, 1904

Costume Study for Nijinsky in His Role in "La Péri"
Léon Bakst, Russian, 1866–1924

Wooded Upland Landscape
Thomas Gainsborough, English, 1727–1788

12

Luigi Vanvitelli, Italian architect, 1700
Edward Lear, English painter, 1812
Dante Gabriel Rossetti, English painter, 1828

13

Henry William Stiegel, American glassmaker, 1729
Georges Braque, French painter, 1882

14

Philippe de Champaigne, French painter, 1602
Thomas Gainsborough, English painter, 1727

15

Richard Avedon, American photographer, 1923
Jasper Johns, American painter, 1930

16

Germain Boffrand, French architect, 1667
John Sell Cotman, English painter, 1782

17

Stefano della Bella, Italian printmaker, 1610

May

18
Carlo Maratti, Italian painter, 1625
Walter Gropius, German architect, 1883
Pierre Balmain, French couturier, 1914

19
Claude Vignon, French painter, 1593
Gaston Lachaise, French sculptor, 1882
Tony Oursler, American video artist, 1957

20
Jacob Jordaens, Flemish painter, 1593
Henri Edmond Cross, French painter, 1856
Jean Dunand, French designer, 1877

21
Albrecht Dürer, German painter, printmaker, 1471
Henri Rousseau, French painter, 1844
Marcel Breuer, American architect, 1902

22
Hubert Robert, French painter, 1733
Marisol, American sculptor, 1930

23
Nicodemus Tessin II, Swedish architect, 1654
Jean Pradier, French sculptor, 1790
Franz Kline, American painter, 1910

The Repast of the Lion
Henri Rousseau, French, 1844–1910

The Road West
Dorothea Lange, American, 1895–1965

24
Emanuel Leutze, American painter, 1816

25
Carlo Dolci, Italian painter, 1616
Mary Cassatt, American painter, 1844

26
Jacopo da Pontormo, Italian painter, 1494
Josef Urban, Austrian architect, set designer, 1872
Dorothea Lange, American photographer, 1895

27
Pierre Legros, French sculptor, 1629
Georges Rouault, French painter, 1871

28
Louis-Jean Desprez, French architect, 1743
Carl Larsson, Swedish illustrator, 1853
Charles Francis Annesley Voysey, English architect, 1857

29
Edme Bouchardon, French sculptor, 1698
George Nelson, American designer, architect, 1908

May–June

30
Peter Carl Fabergé, Russian jeweler, 1846
Alexander Archipenko, Russian sculptor, 1887

31
Walter Sickert, English painter, 1860
Ellsworth Kelly, American painter, 1923

1
Red Grooms, American artist, 1937
Terry Winters, American painter, 1949

2
Francisco Ribalta, Spanish painter, 1565
Albert Besnard, French painter, 1849
Carlo Scarpa, Italian architect, 1906

3
Johan Barthold Jongkind, Dutch painter, 1819
Raoul Dufy, French painter, 1877
Donald Judd, American sculptor, 1928

4

Chance Encounter at 3 A.M.
Red Grooms, American, b. 1937

The Siesta
Paul Gauguin, French, 1848–1903

June

5
Thomas Chippendale, English cabinetmaker, 1718
Édouard Baldus, French photographer, 1813

6
Diego Velázquez, Spanish painter, 1599
Domenico Guidi, Italian sculptor, 1625
Jim Dine, American painter, 1935

7
Paul Gauguin, French painter, 1848
Charles Rennie Mackintosh, Scottish architect, 1868
Damien Hirst, English artist, 1965

8
Sir John Everett Millais, English painter, 1829
Frank Lloyd Wright, American architect, 1867

9
Pieter Saenredam, Dutch painter, 1597

10
Gustave Courbet, French painter, 1819
Fairfield Porter, American painter, 1907

June

11
John Constable, English painter, 1776
Julia Margaret Cameron, English photographer, 1815
Mariano Fortuny y Marsal, Spanish painter, 1838

12
John Roebling, American civil engineer, 1806
Anni Albers, American textile designer, 1899

13
Joseph Stella, American painter, 1877
Marie Vieira da Silva, Portuguese painter, 1908
Christo, American artist, 1935

14
Peter Harrison, American architect, 1716
Margaret Bourke-White, American photographer, 1904
Kevin Roche, American architect, 1922

15
Asher Benjamin, American architect, 1773
Malvina Hoffman, American sculptor, 1885
Saul Steinberg, American illustrator, 1914

16
Filippo Juvarra, Italian architect, 1678
Natalia Gontcharova, French painter, 1881
Irving Penn, American photographer, 1917

Salisbury Cathedral from the Bishop's Grounds
John Constable, English, 1776–1837

Scandinavian Landscape
Allaert van Everdingen, Dutch, 1621–1675

17
André Derain, French painter, 1880
Charles Eames, American designer, 1907

18
Allaert van Everdingen, Dutch painter, 1621
Joseph Marie Vien, French painter, 1716
Robert Walter Weir, American painter, 1803

19
Thomas Sully, American painter, 1783
Charles Gwathmey, American architect, 1938

20
Kurt Schwitters, German collagist, 1887

21
Henry Ossawa Tanner, American painter, 1859
Rockwell Kent, American illustrator, 1882
Paolo Soleri, American architect, 1919

22
Bill Blass, American fashion designer, 1922
Ann Hamilton, American artist, 1956

June

23
Carl Milles, Swedish sculptor, 1875

24
Ferdinand Bol, Dutch painter, 1616
Robert Henri, American painter, 1865

25
Antoni Gaudí, Spanish architect, 1852
Sam Francis, American painter, 1923

26
George Morland, English painter, 1763
Frederick Henry Evans, English photographer, 1853
Barbara Chase-Riboud, American sculptor, 1935

27
Michael Rysbrack, English sculptor, 1693
Charles-Honoré Lannuier, American cabinetmaker, 1779
Philip Guston, American painter, 1913

28
Peter Paul Rubens, Flemish painter, 1577

Mary Fanton Roberts
Robert Henri, American, 1865–1929

The Start of the Race of the Riderless Horses
Émile-Jean-Horace Vernet, French, 1789–1863

29
J. Q. A. Ward, American sculptor, 1830
Robert Laurent, American sculptor, 1890

30
Émile-Jean-Horace Vernet, French painter, 1789
Sean Scully, American painter, 1945

1
Jean Lurçat, French designer, 1892
Ilya Bolotowsky, American painter, 1907

2
André Kertész, American photographer, 1894

3
Robert Adam, English architect, 1728
John Singleton Copley, American painter, 1738
Michael Thonet, Austrian furniture designer, 1796

4
William Rush, American sculptor, 1756
Carolus-Duran, French painter, 1837
Joseph Pennell, American printmaker, 1857

July

5
Chuck Close, American painter, printmaker, 1940

6
John Flaxman, English sculptor, 1755

7
Félicien Rops, Belgian painter, 1833
Marc Chagall, Russian painter, 1887

8
F. Holland Day, American photographer, 1864
Käthe Kollwitz, German printmaker, 1867
Philip Johnson, American architect, 1906

9
Minor White, American photographer, 1908
David Hockney, English painter, 1937

10
Camille Pissarro, French painter, 1830
Giorgio de Chirico, Italian painter, 1888

Still Life with Apples and Pitcher
Camille Pissarro, French, 1830–1903

Reclining Nude
Amedeo Modigliani, Italian, 1884–1920

11
James McNeill Whistler, American painter, 1834
Roger de La Fresnaye, French painter, 1885
Giorgio Armani, Italian fashion designer, 1934

12
Josiah Wedgwood, English potter, 1730
Amedeo Modigliani, Italian painter, 1884
Andrew Wyeth, American painter, 1917

13
Otto Wagner, Austrian architect, 1841

14
Camillo Rusconi, Italian sculptor, 1658
Gustav Klimt, Austrian painter, 1862
Ossip Zadkine, Russian sculptor, 1890

15
Rembrandt, Dutch painter, 1606

16
Andrea del Sarto, Italian painter, 1486
Sir Joshua Reynolds, English painter, 1723
Charles Sheeler, American painter, 1883

July

17
Camille Corot, French painter, 1796
Lyonel Feininger, American painter, 1871
Berenice Abbott, American photographer, 1898

18
Hyacinthe Rigaud, French painter, 1659
Charles James, Anglo-American fashion designer, 1906

19
Inigo Jones, English architect, 1573
John Martin, English painter, 1789
Edgar Degas, French painter, sculptor, printmaker, 1834

20
Max Liebermann, German painter, 1847
Giorgio Morandi, Italian painter, 1890
Lázló Moholy-Nagy, American artist, 1895

21
Sir John Gilbert, English painter, 1817

22
Edward Hopper, American painter, 1882
Alexander Calder, American sculptor, 1898

Office in a Small City
Edward Hopper, American, 1882–1967

The Champion Single Sculls (Max Schmitt in a Single Scull)
Thomas Eakins, American, 1844–1916

23

Wenceslaus Hollar, English printmaker, 1607
Jacques-Germain Soufflot, French architect, 1713
Philipp Otto Runge, German painter, 1777

24

Alexander Jackson Davis, American architect, 1803
Alphonse Mucha, Czech designer, 1860
Alex Katz, American painter, 1927

25

Thomas Eakins, American painter, 1844
Maxfield Parrish, American illustrator, 1870

26

George Catlin, American painter, 1796
George Grosz, German painter, 1893
Andy Goldsworthy, English sculptor, 1956

27

Gilles-Marie Oppenord, French architect, 1672
Louis Vivin, French painter, 1861
Hugo Henneberg, Austrian photographer, 1863

28

Beatrix Potter, English illustrator, 1866
Marcel Duchamp, French painter, 1887
Mel Kendrick, American sculptor, 1949

July–August

29
Francesco Mochi, Italian sculptor, 1580
Hiram Powers, American sculptor, 1805
Eastman Johnson, American painter, 1824

30
Giorgio Vasari, Italian painter, architect, 1511
Henry Moore, English sculptor, 1898

31
Jacques Villon, French painter, 1875
Erich Heckel, German painter, 1883
Jean Dubuffet, French painter, sculptor, 1901

1
Jan van Scorel, Dutch painter, 1495
Richard Wilson, English painter, 1713/4
Yves Saint Laurent, French couturier, 1936

2
Pierre Charles L'Enfant, French urban designer, 1754
John Sloan, American painter, 1871
Arthur Dove, American painter, 1880

3
James Wyatt, English architect, 1746
Joseph Paxton, English architect-engineer, 1801
Pierre Chareau, French architect, 1883

The Lafayette
John Sloan, American, 1871–1951

Arques-la-Bataille
John Henry Twachtman, American, 1853–1902

4
John Henry Twachtman, American painter, 1853

5
Naum Gabo, American sculptor, 1890
I. Rice Pereira, American painter, 1902

6
John Robertson Reid, English painter, 1851
Andy Warhol, American artist, 1928
Howard Hodgkin, English painter, printmaker, 1932

7
Emil Nolde, German painter, 1867

8
Sir Godfrey Kneller, English painter, 1646
Charles Bulfinch, American architect, 1763

9
Pierre-Etienne Monnot, French sculptor, 1657
Eileen Gray, Irish architect, designer, 1879

August

10
Minard Lafever, American architect, 1798
William M. Harnett, American painter, 1848
Reuben Nakian, American sculptor, 1897

11
Martin Johnson Heade, American painter, 1819

12
Thomas Bewick, English printmaker, 1753
Abbott H. Thayer, American painter, 1849
George Bellows, American painter, 1882

13
James Gillray, English illustrator, 1756
George Luks, American painter, 1867
Lorna Simpson, American sculptor, 1960

14
Joseph Vernet, French painter, 1714

15
Agostino Carracci, Italian painter, 1557
Francesco Zuccarelli, Italian painter, 1702
Walter Crane, English illustrator, 1845

Ox Team, Matinicus Island, Maine
George Bellows, American, 1882–1925

Broken Eggs
Jean Baptiste Greuze, French, 1725–1805

16

17
Bessie Potter Vonnoh, American sculptor, 1872
Larry Rivers, American painter, 1923

18
Gustave Caillebotte, French painter, 1848
Giacomo Balla, Italian painter, sculptor, 1871
Pietro Belluschi, American architect, 1899

19
Coco Chanel, French couturiere, 1883
Bradley Walker Tomlin, American painter, 1899

20
Eliel Saarinen, Finnish architect, 1873
Eero Saarinen, American architect, 1910
Bernd Becher, American photographer, 1931

21
Jean Baptiste Greuze, French painter, 1725
Asher B. Durand, American painter, 1796
Narcisse Diaz de la Peña, French painter, 1808

August

22
Charles Percier, French architect, 1764
Jacques Lipchitz, French sculptor, 1891
Henri Cartier-Bresson, French photographer, 1908

23

24
Charles McKim, American architect, 1847

25
Sassoferrato, Italian painter, 1609
Jacob Maris, Dutch painter, 1837
Man Ray, American painter, photographer, 1890

26

27

Banks of the River Marne
Henri Cartier-Bresson, French, 1908–2004

The Death of Socrates
Jacques-Louis David, French, 1748–1825

August–September

28
Constant Troyon, French painter, 1810
Sir Edward Burne-Jones, English painter, 1833
Morris Graves, American painter, 1910

29
J. A. D. Ingres, French painter, 1780
John Leech, English illustrator, 1817

30
Jacques-Louis David, French painter, 1748
J. Alden Weir, American painter, 1852
Theo van Doesburg, Dutch painter, 1883

31
Georg Jensen, Danish silversmith, 1866

1
Yasuo Kuniyoshi, American painter, 1893

2
Louis Séraphine, French painter, 1864
Romare Bearden, American painter, 1911
Hilla Becher, German photographer, 1934

September

3
Louis Sullivan, American architect, 1856

4
Thomas U. Walter, American architect, 1804
Daniel Burnham, American architect, 1846
Oskar Schlemmer, German painter, sculptor, 1888

5
Maurice-Quentin de La Tour, French painter, 1704
Caspar David Friedrich, German painter, 1774
Rudolph Schindler, American architect, 1887

6
Sebastiano Serlio, Italian architect, 1475
Horatio Greenough, American sculptor, 1805
Georges de Feure, French designer, 1868

7
William Butterfield, English architect, 1814
Grandma Moses, American painter, 1860
Jacob Lawrence, American painter, 1917

8

The Photographer
Jacob Lawrence, American, 1917–2000

The Eiffel Tower at Twilight
Brassaï, French (b. Transylvania), 1899–1984

9
Brassaï, French photographer, 1899

10
Sir John Soane, English architect, 1753

11
William Holabird, American architect, 1854

12
Anselm Feuerbach, German painter, 1829
Ben Shahn, American painter, 1898
Nan Goldin, American photographer, 1953

13
Robert Indiana, American painter, 1928
Tadao Andō, Japanese architect, 1941

14
Sir Peter Lely, English painter, 1618
Jeremiah Dummer, American silversmith, 1645
Charles Dana Gibson, American illustrator, 1867

September

15
Jean Jacques Grandville, French printmaker, 1803

16
Jean Arp, French sculptor, 1887
Carl André, American sculptor, 1935

17
Jean-Baptiste Le Prince, French printmaker, 1734
Samuel Prout, English painter, 1783

18
José de Rivera, American sculptor, 1904
Mark di Suvero, American sculptor, 1933

19
Arthur Rackham, English illustrator, 1867

20
Pierre Léonard Fontaine, French architect, 1762
Théodore Chassériau, French painter, 1819
Dale Chihuly, American glass artist, 1941

The Cow Jumped over the Moon
Arthur Rackham, English, 1867–1939

Italian Hill Town
Arthur B. Davies, American, 1862–1928

September

21
Julio Gonzáles, Spanish sculptor, 1876
Pavel Tchelitchew, American painter, 1898
Hans Hartung, French painter, 1904

22
František Kupka, Czech painter, 1871
Erik Gunnar Asplund, Swedish architect, designer, 1885

23
Joseph-Siffred Duplessis, French painter, 1725
Matthew Pratt, American painter, 1734
Paul Delvaux, Belgian painter, 1897

24
Horace Walpole, English connoisseur, 1717
Antoine-Louis Barye, French sculptor, 1795

25
Francesco Borromini, Italian architect, 1599
Mark Rothko, American painter, 1903

26
Théodore Géricault, French painter, 1791
Arthur B. Davies, American painter, 1862
Lewis W. Hine, American photographer, 1874

September–October

27
René-Michel Slodtz, French sculptor, 1705
George Cruikshank, English caricaturist, 1792
Thomas Nast, American cartoonist, 1840

28
Caravaggio, Italian painter, 1571
Frederick William MacMonnies, American sculptor, 1863
David Salle, American printmaker, 1952

29
Antoine Coysevox, French sculptor, 1640
François Boucher, French painter, 1703
Henry Hobson Richardson, American architect, 1838

30
Petah Coyne, American sculptor, 1953

1
Jacopo Barozzi da Vignola, Italian architect, 1507
Nicolaes Berchem, Dutch painter, 1620
Larry Poons, American painter, 1937

2

The Musicians
Caravaggio, Italian (Lombard), 1571–1610

Piazza San Marco
Francesco Guardi, Italian (Venetian), 1712–1793

3
Pierre Bonnard, French painter, 1867
Laurie Simmons, American photographer, 1949

4
Giovanni Battista Piranesi, Italian printmaker, 1720
Jean François Millet, French painter, 1814
Frederic Remington, American artist, 1861

5
Francesco Guardi, Italian painter, 1712
Thomas Anshutz, American painter, 1851

6
Adolf von Hildebrand, German sculptor, 1847
Frank M. Sutcliffe, English photographer, 1853
Le Corbusier, Swiss architect, 1887

7

8
Cornelis Troost, Dutch painter, 1696
Aristide Maillol, French sculptor, 1861
Faith Ringgold, American painter, 1930

October

9
Louis-Simon Boizot, French sculptor, 1743
Frank Duveneck, American painter, 1848

10
Antoine Watteau, French painter, 1684
Alberto Giacometti, Swiss sculptor, 1901
Chris Ofili, British artist, 1968

11
James Barry, English painter, 1741

12
Al Held, American painter, 1928

13
Mariotto Albertinelli, Italian painter, 1474

14
Alesso Baldovinetti, Italian painter, 1425

Studies of a Woman Wearing a Cap
Antoine Watteau, French, 1684–1721

Street in Portsmouth
Childe Hassam, American, 1859–1935

15

John Vanderlyn, American painter, 1775
James Tissot, French painter, 1836
Ralph Blakelock, American painter, 1847

16

Pierre Puget, French sculptor, 1620
Paul Strand, American photographer, 1890

17

Canaletto, Italian painter, 1697
Jean-Baptiste Regnault, French painter, 1754
Childe Hassam, American painter, 1859

18

Luca Giordano, Italian painter, 1634

19

Arnold Böcklin, Swiss painter, 1827
Umberto Boccioni, Italian sculptor, 1882

20

Andrea della Robbia, Italian sculptor, 1435
Sir Christopher Wren, English architect, 1632

October

21
Katsushika Hokusai, Japanese printmaker, 1760

22
Harry Callahan, American photographer, 1912
Robert Rauschenberg, American painter, 1925
Raghubir Singh, Indian photographer, 1942

23
Wilhelm Leibl, German painter, 1844
Jean-Louis Forain, French illustrator, 1852
Paul Cret, American architect, 1876

24
Eugène Fromentin, French painter, 1820
Mainbocher, American couturier, 1890

25
Richard Parkes Bonington, English painter, 1802
Pablo Picasso, Spanish artist, 1881

26
Vasily Vereshchagin, Russian painter, 1842
Julian Schnabel, American painter, 1951

The Great Wave off Kanagawa
Katsushika Hokusai, Japanese, 1760–1849

Young Woman with a Water Pitcher
Johannes Vermeer, Dutch, 1632–1675

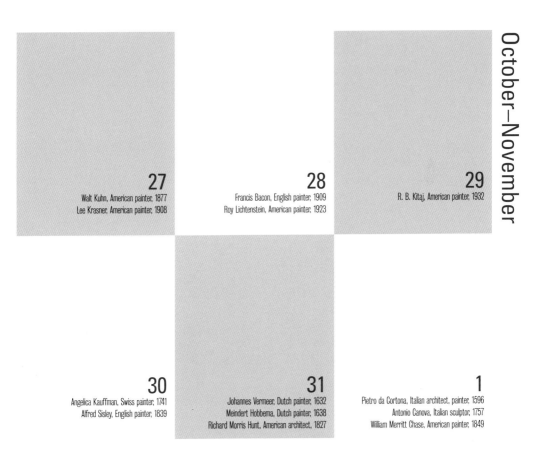

October–November

27
Walt Kuhn, American painter, 1877
Lee Krasner, American painter, 1908

28
Francis Bacon, English painter, 1909
Roy Lichtenstein, American painter, 1923

29
R. B. Kitaj, American painter, 1932

30
Angelica Kauffman, Swiss painter, 1741
Alfred Sisley, English painter, 1839

31
Johannes Vermeer, Dutch painter, 1632
Meindert Hobbema, Dutch painter, 1638
Richard Morris Hunt, American architect, 1827

1
Pietro da Cortona, Italian architect, painter, 1596
Antonio Canova, Italian sculptor, 1757
William Merritt Chase, American painter, 1849

November

2
Jean-Siméon Chardin, French painter, 1699
Richard Serra, American sculptor, 1939

3
Benvenuto Cellini, Italian goldsmith, sculptor, 1500
Annibale Carracci, Italian painter, 1560
Walker Evans, American photographer, 1903

4
Guido Reni, Italian painter, 1575
Charles Despiau, French sculptor, 1874
Robert Mapplethorpe, American photographer, 1946

5
Philips Koninck, Dutch painter, 1619
Washington Allston, American painter, 1779
Raymond Duchamp-Villon, French sculptor, 1876

6
J. N. F. Alois Senefelder, German lithographer, 1771
Adolphe Sax, Belgian saxophone maker, 1814
Charles Garnier, French architect, 1825

7
Francisco de Zurbarán, Spanish painter, 1598

People in Downtown Havana
Walker Evans, American, 1903–1975

Red Poppies
Charles Demuth, American, 1883–1935

8

Andrea Palladio, Italian architect, 1508
Charles Demuth, American painter, 1883

9

Stanford White, American architect, 1853

10

William Hogarth, English painter, engraver, 1697
Sir Jacob Epstein, English sculptor, 1880
Erté, Russian designer, 1892

11

Frans Snyders, Flemish painter, 1579
Paul Signac, French painter, 1863
Édouard Vuillard, French painter, 1868

12

Frank Furness, American architect, 1839
Auguste Rodin, French sculptor, 1840

13

November

14
Johann Lukas von Hildebrandt, Austrian architect, 1668
Claude Monet, French painter, 1840
John Steuart Curry, American painter, 1897

15
Robert Le Lorrain, French sculptor, 1666
Georgia O'Keeffe, American painter, 1887
Wayne Thiebaud, American painter, 1920

16
Francis Danby, English painter, 1793

17
Agnolo Bronzino, Italian painter, 1503
Sir Charles Eastlake, English painter, 1793
Isamu Noguchi, American sculptor, 1904

18
Gaspar de Crayer, Flemish painter, 1584
Sir David Wilkie, Scottish painter, 1785
L. J. M. Daguerre, French photographer, 1787

19
Eustache Le Sueur, French painter, 1616
Bertel Thorvaldsen, Danish sculptor, 1768/70

Landscape: The Parc Monceau
Claude Monet, French, 1840–1926

Cover for L'Estampe Originale
Henri de Toulouse-Lautrec, French, 1864–1901

20

Paulus Potter, Dutch painter, 1625
Bartolomeo Pinelli, Italian designer, 1781

21

René Magritte, Belgian painter, 1898

22

Ignaz Günther, German sculptor, 1725
Copley Fielding (Anthony Vandyke), English painter, 1787
Francis W. Edmonds, American painter, 1806

23

José Orozco, Mexican painter, 1883
El Lissitzky, Russian artist, 1890
Donald Deskey, American industrial designer, 1894

24

John Bacon, English sculptor, 1740
Cass Gilbert, American architect, 1859
Henri de Toulouse-Lautrec, French painter, printmaker, 1864

25

Maurice Denis, French painter, 1870

26
William Sidney Mount, American painter, 1807
George Segal, American sculptor, 1924
Kara Walker, American artist, 1969

27
José de Creeft, American sculptor, 1884
Tsugouharu Foujita, Japanese painter, 1886

28
William Blake, English painter, 1757
Morris Louis, American painter, 1912

29
James Rosenquist, American painter, 1933

30
Adriaen van de Velde, Dutch painter, 1636
Adolphe-William Bouguereau, French painter, 1825

1
Étienne-Maurice Falconet, French sculptor, 1716

Cider Making
William Sidney Mount, American, 1807–1868

Study for "A Sunday on La Grande Jatte"
Georges-Pierre Seurat, French, 1859–1891

2

Georges-Pierre Seurat, French painter, 1859
Otto Dix, German painter, 1891
Gianni Versace, Italian fashion designer, 1946

3

Gilbert Stuart, American painter, 1755

4

Wassily Kandinsky, Russian painter, 1866
Gae Aulenti, Italian architect, designer, 1927

5

Pierre-Philippe Thomire, French sculptor, 1751
Walt Disney, American film cartoonist, 1901

6

Frédéric Bazille, French painter, 1841
Karl Bitter, American sculptor, 1867
Eliot Porter, American photographer, 1901

7

Gian Lorenzo Bernini, Italian sculptor, architect, 1598
Stuart Davis, American painter, 1892

December

8
Albert Gleizes, French painter, 1881
Lucian Freud, English painter, printmaker, 1922

9
Roy DeCarava, American photographer, 1919

10
Adriaen van Ostade, Dutch painter, 1610
Adolph Loos, Austrian architect, 1870

11
Mark Tobey, American painter, 1890

12
Edvard Munch, Norwegian painter, printmaker, 1863
Helen Frankenthaler, American painter, 1928

13
Clark Mills, American sculptor, 1810
Diego Rivera, Mexican painter, 1886
Antonio Tàpies, Spanish painter, 1923

Mystical Shore
Edvard Munch, Norwegian, 1863–1944

Guardroom with the Deliverance of Saint Peter
David Teniers the Younger, Flemish, 1610–1690

December

14
François Hubert Drouais, French painter, 1727
Puvis de Chavannes, French painter, 1824

15
David Teniers the Younger, Flemish painter, 1610
Oscar Niemeyer, Brazilian architect, 1907

16
Edward Ruscha, American painter, filmmaker, 1937

17
François-Marius Granet, French painter, 1775
Paul César Helleu, French painter, 1859
Paul Cadmus, American painter, 1904

18
Paul Klee, German painter, 1879
Walter Dorwin Teague, American designer, 1883

19
Fitz Hugh Lane, American painter, 1804

December

20
Pieter de Hooch, Dutch painter, 1629
Clodion, French sculptor, 1738
Calvert Vaux, American architect, 1824

21
Masaccio, Italian painter, 1401
Thomas Couture, French painter, 1815

22
John Crome, English painter, 1768
Giacomo Manzù, Italian sculptor, 1908
Jean-Michel Basquiat, American painter, printmaker, 1960

23
George Barnard, American photographer, 1819
John Marin, American painter, 1870
Nancy Graves, American painter, sculptor, 1940

24
Abraham Bloemaert, Dutch painter, 1566
Joseph Cornell, American sculptor, 1903
Ad Reinhardt, American painter, 1913

25
Paul Manship, American sculptor, 1885
Raphael Soyer, American painter, 1899
Louise Bourgeois, American sculptor, 1911

Lower Manhattan from the River, Number 1
John Marin, American, 1870–1953

The Port of Honfleur at Night
Félix Vallotton, French (b. Switzerland), 1865–1925

December

26
George Romney, English painter, 1734

27

28
Thomas Hovenden, American painter, 1840
Felix Vallotton, French painter, 1865

29
Jean Baptiste Pater, French painter, 1695

30
W. Eugene Smith, American photographer, 1918

31
Giovanni Boldini, Italian painter, 1845
Henri Matisse, French painter, 1869
Max Pechstein, German painter, 1881

CREDITS

All of the works reproduced in this book are from the collection of The Metropolitan Museum of Art.

COVER

Morning Glories (detail)
Suzuki Kiitsu, Japanese, 1796–1858
One of a pair of six-panel folding screens
Ink, color, and gold on gilded paper, 6 ft. x 13 ft., early 19th century
Seymour Fund, 1954 54.69.2

TITLE PAGE

Four Cakes
Wayne Thiebaud, American, b. 1920
From *Recent Etchings I*
Etching and aquatint, 16 15/16 x 23 13/16 in., 1979
Gift of The Kronos Collections, 1982 1982.1164.6

INTRODUCTION

Washington Crossing the Delaware
Emanuel Leutze, American, 1816–1868
Oil on canvas, 12 ft. 5 in. x 21 ft. 3 in., 1851
Gift of John Stewart Kennedy, 1897 97.34

An Icy Night
Alfred Stieglitz, American, 1864–1946
Gelatin silver print from glass negative, 3⅝ x 4⅝ in., 1898, printed 1920s
Alfred Stieglitz Collection, 1949 49.55.7

Two Girls on a Lawn
John Singer Sargent, American, 1856–1925
Oil on canvas, 21⅛ x 25¼ in., ca. 1889
Gift of Mrs. Francis Ormond, 1950 50.130.20

Still Life with Roses and Fruit
Henri Fantin-Latour, French, 1836–1904
Oil on canvas, 13⅝ x 16⅜ in., 1863
Bequest of Alice A. Hay, 1987 1987.119

Apples
Paul Cézanne, French, 1839–1906
Oil on canvas, 9 x 13 in., 1878–79
The Mr. and Mrs. Henry Ittleson Jr. Purchase Fund, 1961 61.103

Merengue en Boca Chica
Rafael Ferrer, American (b. Puerto Rico), b. 1933
Oil on canvas, 60 x 72 in., 1983
Purchase, Anonymous Gift, 1984 1984.2

Three Women by a Garden
Fernand Léger, French, 1881–1955
Oil on canvas, 25½ x 36 in., 1922
Bequest of Mr. and Mrs. Allan D. Emil, in honor of William S. Lieberman, 1987 1987.125.1

The Tomb of Sir Walter Scott in Dryburgh Abbey
William Henry Fox Talbot, English, 1800–1877
Salted paper print from paper negative, 6⅝ x 7 1/16 in., 1844
The Rubel Collection, Purchase, Lila Acheson Wallace and Jennifer and Joseph Duke Gifts, 1997 1997.382.4

Still Life with Cake
Raphaelle Peale, American, 1774–1825
Oil on wood, 10¾ x 15¼ in., 1818
Maria DeWitt Jesup Fund, 1959 59.166

Victorian Interior II
Horace Pippin, American, 1888–1946
Oil on canvas, 25¼ x 30 in., 1945
Arthur Hoppock Hearn Fund, 1958 58.26

A Wall, Nassau
Winslow Homer, American, 1836–1910
Watercolor and graphite on off-white wove paper, 14⅞ x 21⅜ in., 1898
Amelia B. Lazarus Fund, 1910 10.228.9

Studies for the Libyan Sibyl
Michelangelo Buonarroti, Italian (Florentine), 1475–1564
Red chalk, 11⅜ x 8 7/16 in., 1508–12
Purchase, Joseph Pulitzer Bequest, 1924 24.197.2

The Steeplechase, Coney Island
Milton Avery, American, 1885–1965
Oil on canvas, 32 x 40 in., 1929
Gift of Sally M. Avery, 1984 1984.527

The Green Car
William Glackens, American, 1870–1938
Oil on canvas, 24 x 32 in., 1910
Arthur Hoppock Hearn Fund, 1937 37.73

Still Life with a Guitar
Juan Gris, Spanish, 1887–1927
Oil on canvas, 26 x 39½ in., 1913
Jacques and Natasha Gelman Collection, 1998 1999.363.28

Oleanders
Vincent van Gogh, Dutch, 1853–1890
Oil on canvas, 23¾ x 29 in., 1888
Gift of Mr. and Mrs. John L. Loeb, 1962 62.24

Portrait of a Woman with a Dog
Jean Honoré Fragonard, French, 1732–1806
Oil on canvas, 32 x 25¾ in., about 1769
Fletcher Fund, 1937 37.118

Mirror Lake—Valley of the Yosemite
Eadweard Muybridge, American (b. England), 1830–1904
Albumen silver print from glass negative, printed by Bradley and Rulofson, 16⅞ x 21⅜ in., 1872
David Hunter McAlpin Fund, 1966 66.724.2

A Bear Walking
Leonardo da Vinci, Italian (Florentine), 1452–1519
Metalpoint on light buff prepared paper, 4 1/16 x 5¼ in., ca. 1490
Robert Lehman Collection, 1975 1975.1.369

Animated Landscape
Joan Miró, Spanish, 1893–1983
Oil on canvas, 51 x 76¾ in., 1927
Jacques and Natasha Gelman Collection, 1998 1999.363.49

Basket of Flowers
Eugène Delacroix, French, 1798–1863
Oil on canvas, 42¼ x 56 in., 1848–49
Bequest of Miss Adelaide Milton de Groot (1876–1967), 1967 67.187.60

Autumn Oaks
George Inness, American, 1825–1894
Oil on canvas, 20⅜ x 30⅛ in., ca. 1878
Gift of George I. Seney, 1887 87.8.8

Costume Study for Nijinsky in His Role in "La Péri"
Léon Bakst, Russian, 1866–1924
Watercolor and gold and silver paints over graphite, 26⅝ x 19¼ in., 1922
Gift of Sir Joseph Duveen, 1922 22.226.1

Wooded Upland Landscape
Thomas Gainsborough, English, 1727–1788
Oil on canvas, 47⅜ x 58⅛ in., probably 1783
Gift of George A. Hearn, 1906 06.1279

The Repast of the Lion
Henri Rousseau, French, 1844–1910
Oil on canvas, 44¾ x 63 in., ca. 1907
Bequest of Sam A. Lewisohn, 1951 51.112.5

The Road West
Dorothea Lange, American, 1895–1965
Gelatin silver print, 6 13/16 x 9 7/16 in., 1938
Purchase, The Horace W. Goldsmith Foundation Gift and Harriette and Noel Levine Gift, 1990 1990.1005

Chance Encounter at 3 A.M.
Red Grooms, American, b. 1937
Oil on canvas, 8 ft. 4 in. x 12 ft. 11 in., 1984
Purchase, Mr. and Mrs. Wolfgang Schoenborn Gift, 1984 1984.194

The Siesta
Paul Gauguin, French, 1848–1903
Oil on canvas, 35 x 45¾ in., ca. 1892–94
The Walter H. and Leonore Annenberg Collection, Gift of Walter H. and Leonore Annenberg, 1993, Bequest of Walter H. Annenberg, 2002 1993.400.3

Salisbury Cathedral from the Bishop's Grounds
John Constable, English, 1776–1837
Oil on canvas, 34⅝ x 44 in., ca. 1825
Bequest of Mary Stillman Harkness, 1950 50.145.8

Scandinavian Landscape
Allaert van Everdingen, Dutch, 1621–1675
Watercolor on paper, 5⅝ x 7⅝ in.
Rogers Fund, 1966 66.134.2

Mary Fanton Roberts
Robert Henri, American, 1865–1929
Oil on canvas, 32 x 26 in., 1917
Bequest of Mary Fanton Roberts, 1956 57.45

The Start of the Race of the Riderless Horses
Émile-Jean-Horace Vernet, French, 1789–1863
Oil on canvas, 18⅛ x 21¼ in., by 1820
Catharine Lorillard Wolfe Collection, Bequest of Catharine Lorillard Wolfe, 1887 87.15.47

Still Life with Apples and Pitcher
Camille Pissarro, French, 1830–1903
Oil on canvas, 18¼ x 22¼ in., 1872
Purchase, Mr. and Mrs. Richard J. Bernhard Gift, by exchange, 1983 1983.166

Reclining Nude
Amedeo Modigliani, Italian, 1884–1920
Oil on canvas, 23⅞ x 36½ in., 1917
The Mr. and Mrs. Klaus G. Perls Collection, 1997 1997.149.9

Office in a Small City
Edward Hopper, American, 1882–1967
Oil on canvas, 28 x 40 in., 1953
George A. Hearn Fund, 1953 53.183

The Champion Single Sculls (Max Schmitt in a Single Scull)
Thomas Eakins, American, 1844–1916
Oil on canvas, 32¼ x 46¼ in., 1871
Purchase, The Alfred N. Punnett Endowment Fund and George D. Pratt Gift, 1934 34.92

The Lafayette
John Sloan, American, 1871–1951
Oil on canvas, 30½ x 36⅛ in., 1927
Gift of The Friends of John Sloan, 1928 28.18

Arques-la-Bataille
John Henry Twachtman, American, 1853–1902
Oil on canvas, 60 x 78⅞ in., 1885
Morris K. Jesup Fund, 1968 68.52

Ox Team, Matinicus Island, Maine
George Bellows, American, 1882–1925
Oil on wood, 22 x 28 in., 1916
Gift of Mr. and Mrs. Raymond J. Horowitz, 1974
1974.352

Broken Eggs
Jean Baptiste Greuze, French, 1725–1805
Oil on canvas, 28¾ x 37 in., 1756
Bequest of William K. Vanderbilt, 1920 20.155.8

Banks of the River Marne
Henri Cartier-Bresson, French, 1908–2004
Gelatin silver print, 9¾ x 14 9/16 in., 1938
Gift of Grace and Andrew Schoelkopf, 2002
2002.614.1

The Death of Socrates
Jacques-Louis David, French, 1748–1825
Oil on canvas, 51 x 77¼ in., 1787
Catharine Lorillard Wolfe Collection, Wolfe Fund,
1931 31.45

The Photographer
Jacob Lawrence, American, 1917–2000
Watercolor, gouache, and pencil on paper,
22⅛ x 30½ in., 1942
Purchase, Lila Acheson Wallace Gift, 2001 2001.205

The Eiffel Tower at Twilight
Brassaï, French (b. Transylvania), 1899–1984
Gelatin silver print, 11 5/16 x 8 13/16 in., ca. 1932
Gift of the artist, 1980 1980.1029.4

The Cow Jumped over the Moon
Arthur Rackham, English, 1867–1939
From *Mother Goose: The Old Nursery Rhymes*
Published by the Century Co., New York
Commercial printing, 9½ x 7¼ in., 1913
Gift of Fairchild Bowler, 1965 65.518.15

Italian Hill Town
Arthur B. Davies, American, 1862–1928
Oil on canvas, 25⅞ x 39⅞ in., ca. 1925
Bequest of Lizzie P. Bliss, 1931 31.67.3

The Musicians
Caravaggio (Michelangelo Merisi), Italian (Lombard),
1571–1610
Oil on canvas, 36¼ x 46⅝ in., ca. 1595
Rogers Fund, 1952 52.81

Piazza San Marco
Francesco Guardi, Italian (Venetian), 1712–1793
Oil on canvas, 27⅛ x 33¾ in., probably 1750s
Bequest of Mary Stillman Harkness, 1950 50.145.21

Studies of a Woman Wearing a Cap
Antoine Watteau, French, 1684–1721
Black, red, and white chalk on paper, 7¼ x 8 1/16 in., ca.
1717–18
Bequest of Therese Kuhn Straus, in memory of her
husband, Herbert N. Straus, 1978 1978.12.3

Street in Portsmouth
Childe Hassam, American, 1859–1935
Watercolor on off-white wove paper, 15⅛ x 22 in.,
1916
Rogers Fund, 1917 17.31.2

The Great Wave off Kanagawa
Katsushika Hokusai, Japanese, 1760–1849
From the series *Thirty-six Views of Mount Fuji*
Color woodblock print, 10⅛ x 14 15/16 in., 1830–32
H. O. Havemeyer Collection, Bequest of Mrs. H. O.
Havemeyer, 1929 JP 1847

Young Woman with a Water Pitcher
Johannes Vermeer, Dutch, 1632–1675
Oil on canvas, 18 x 16 in., ca. 1662
Marquand Collection, Gift of Henry G. Marquand,
1889 89.15.21

People in Downtown Havana
Walker Evans, American, 1903–1975
Gelatin silver print, 5 15/16 x 9 in., 1933
Gift of Lincoln Kirstein, 1952 52.562.7

Red Poppies
Charles Demuth, American, 1883–1935
Watercolor and pencil on paper, 13⅞ x 19⅞ in., 1929
Gift of Henry and Louise Loeb, 1983 1983.40

Landscape: The Parc Monceau
Claude Monet, French, 1840–1926
Oil on canvas, 23½ x 32½ in., 1876
Bequest of Loula D. Lasker, New York City, 1961
59.206

Cover for L'Estampe Originale
Henri de Toulouse-Lautrec, French, 1864–1901
Color lithograph, 17¾ x 23¾ in., 1893
Rogers Fund, 1922 22.82.1 (1)

Cider Making
William Sidney Mount, American, 1807–1868
Oil on canvas, 27 x 34⅛ in., 1840–41
Purchase, Bequest of Charles Allen Munn, by
exchange, 1966 66.126

Study for "A Sunday on La Grande Jatte"
Georges-Pierre Seurat, French, 1859–1891
Oil on canvas, 27¾ x 41 in., 1884–85
Bequest of Sam A. Lewisohn, 1951 51.112.6

Mystical Shore
Edvard Munch, Norwegian, 1863–1944
Woodcut printed in green, 14⅜ x 22½ in., 1897
Bequest of Scofield Thayer, 1982 1984.1203.9

Guardroom with the Deliverance of Saint Peter
David Teniers the Younger, Flemish, 1610–1690
Oil on wood, 21¼ x 29⅝ in., ca. 1645–47
Anonymous Gift, 1964 64.65.5

Lower Manhattan from the River, Number 1
John Marin, American, 1870–1953
Watercolor, charcoal, and graphite on paper,
21¾ x 26½ in., 1921
Alfred Stieglitz Collection, 1949 49.70.122

The Port of Honfleur at Night
Félix Vallotton, French (b. Switzerland), 1865–1925
Oil on cardboard, 27½ x 39¾ in., 1901
Bequest of Miss Adelaide Milton de Groot
(1876–1967), 1967 67.187.116

Bonheur, Rosa, *March 16*
Bonington, Richard Parkes, *October 25*
Bonnard, Pierre, *October 3*
Borromini, Francesco, *September 25*
Botero, Fernando, *April 19*
Botta, Mario, *April 1*
Bouchardon, Edme, *May 29*
Boucher, François, *September 29*
Bouguereau, Adolphe-William, *November 30*
Bourdon, Sébastien, *February 2*
Bourgeois, Louise, *December 25*
Bourke-White, Margaret, *June 14*
Brancusi, Constantin, *February 19*
Braque, Georges, *May 13*
Brassaï, *September 9*
Bravo, Manuel Alvarez, *February 4*
Breton, Jules, *May 1*
Breuer, Marcel, *May 21*
Bronzino, Agnolo, *November 17*
Brown, George Loring, *February 2*
Bulfinch, Charles, *August 8*
Bullock, Wynn, *April 18*
Bunshaft, Gordon, *May 9*
Burchfield, Charles, *April 9*
Burne-Jones, Sir Edward, *August 28*
Burnham, Daniel, *September 4*
Butterfield, William, *September 7*

C

Cadmus, Paul, *December 17*
Caffiéri, Jean-Jacques, *April 30*
Caillebotte, Gustave, *August 18*
Calder, Alexander, *July 22*
Calder, Alexander Stirling, *January 11*
Callahan, Harry, *October 22*
Cameron, Julia Margaret, *June 11*
Canaletto, *October 17*
Canova, Antonio, *November 1*
Caravaggio, *September 28*
Caresme, Jacques-Philippe, *February 25*
Caro, Anthony, *March 28*
Carolus-Duran, *July 4*
Carpeaux, Jean-Baptiste, *May 11*
Carrà, Carlo, *February 11*
Carracci, Agostino, *August 15*
Carracci, Annibale, *November 3*
Carracci, Ludovico, *April 19*
Carrière, Eugène, *January 27*
Carroll, Lewis, *January 27*
Cartier-Bresson, Henri, *August 22*
Cassatt, Mary, *May 25*
Catlin, George, *July 26*
Cellini, Benvenuto, *November 3*
Cerquozzi, Michelangelo, *February 18*
Cézanne, Paul, *January 19*
Chagall, Marc, *July 7*
Chamberlain, John, *April 16*
Chambers, Sir William, *February 23*

Champaigne, Philippe de, *May 14*
Chanel, Coco, *August 19*
Chardin, Jean-Siméon, *November 2*
Chareau, Pierre, *August 3*
Chase, William Merritt, *November 1*
Chase-Riboud, Barbara, *June 26*
Chassériau, Théodore, *September 20*
Chavannes, Puvis de, *December 14*
Chihuly, Dale, *September 20*
Chippendale, Thomas, *June 5*
Chirico, Giorgio de, *July 10*
Christo, *June 13*
Church, Frederic Edwin, *May 4*
Clemente, Francesco, *March 23*
Clodion, *December 20*
Close, Chuck, *July 5*
Cochin, Charles-Nicolas, II, *February 22*
Coe, Sue, *February 21*
Cole, Thomas, *February 1*
Coninxloo, Gillis van, *January 24*
Constable, John, *June 11*
Copley, John Singleton, *July 3*
Corbusier, Le, *October 6*
Cornell, Joseph, *December 24*
Corot, Camille, *July 17*
Cortona, Pietro da, *November 1*
Cotman, John Sell, *May 16*
Courbet, Gustave, *June 10*
Courrèges, André, *March 9*
Coustou, Nicolas, *January 9*

Couture, Thomas, *December 21*
Cox, David, *April 29*
Coyne, Petah, *September 30*
Coysevox, Antoine, *September 29*
Crane, Walter, *August 15*
Crawford, Thomas, *March 22*
Crayer, Gaspar de, *November 18*
Creeft, José de, *November 27*
Cret, Paul, *October 23*
Cristofori, Bartolomeo, *May 4*
Crome, John, *December 22*
Cross, Henri Edmond, *May 20*
Cruikshank, George, *September 27*
Cunningham, Imogen, *April 12*
Curry, John Steuart, *November 14*

D

Dagnan-Bouveret, P. A. J., *January 7*
Daguerre, L. J. M., *November 18*
Dalí, Salvador, *May 11*
Danby, Francis, *November 16*
Daubigny, Charles-François, *February 15*
Daumier, Honoré, *February 26*
David, Jacques-Louis, *August 30*
David d'Angers, *March 12*
Davies, Arthur B., *September 26*
Davis, Alexander Jackson, *July 24*

Davis, Stuart, *December 7*
Day, F. Holland, *July 8*
De Kooning, Willem, *April 24*
De Rivera, José, *September 18*
Debucourt, Philibert-Louis, *February 13*
Decamps, Alexandre-Gabriel, *May 3*
DeCarava, Roy, *December 9*
Degas, Edgar, *July 19*
Del Sarto, Andrea, *July 16*
Delacroix, Eugène, *April 26*
Delaunay, Robert, *April 12*
Delvaux, Laurent, *January 17*
Delvaux, Paul, *September 23*
Demuth, Charles, *November 8*
Denis, Maurice, *November 25*
Derain, André, *June 17*
Deskey, Donald, *November 23*
Despiau, Charles, *November 4*
Desprez, Louis-Jean, *May 28*
Di Suvero, Mark, *September 18*
Diaz de la Peña, Narcisse, *August 21*
Diebenkorn, Richard, *April 22*
Dine, Jim, *June 6*
Dior, Christian, *January 21*
Disney, Walt, *December 5*
Dix, Otto, *December 2*
Doesburg, Theo van, *August 30*
Dolci, Carlo, *May 25*
Dongen, Kees van, *January 26*
Donner, Georg Raphael, *April 25*

Doré, Gustave, *January 6*
Dou, Gerard, *April 7*
Dove, Arthur, *August 2*
Drouais, François Hubert, *December 14*
Dubuffet, Jean, *July 31*
Duchamp, Marcel, *July 28*
Duchamp-Villon, Raymond, *November 5*
Dufy, Raoul, *June 3*
Dummer, Jeremiah, *September 14*
Dunand, Jean, *May 20*
Duplessis, Joseph-Siffred, *September 23*
Dupré, Jules, *April 5*
Durand, Asher B., *August 21*
Dürer, Albrecht, *May 21*
Duveneck, Frank, *October 9*
Dyck, Anthony van, *March 22*

E

Eakins, Thomas, *July 25*
Eames, Charles, *June 17*
Eastlake, Charles Lock, *March 11*
Eastlake, Sir Charles, *November 17*
Edmonds, Francis W., *November 22*
Elsheimer, Adam, *March 18*
Ensor, James, *April 13*
Epstein, Sir Jacob, *November 10*
Ernst, Max, *April 2*

Erté, *November 10*
Etty, William, *March 10*
Evans, Frederick Henry, *June 26*
Evans, Walker, *November 3*
Everdingen, Allaert van, *June 18*

F

Fabergé, Peter Carl, *May 30*
Falconet, Étienne-Maurice, *December 1*
Fantin-Latour, Henri, *January 14*
Feininger, Lyonel, *July 17*
Ferrer, Rafael, *January 25*
Feuerbach, Anselm, *September 12*
Feure, Georges de, *September 6*
Fielding, Copley (Anthony Vandyke),
  November 22
Fiorentino, Rosso, *March 8*
Flannagan, John B., *April 7*
Flavin, Dan, *April 1*
Flaxman, John, *July 6*
Foggini, Giovanni Battista, *April 25*
Fontaine, Pierre Léonard, *September 20*
Fontana, Lucio, *February 19*
Forain, Jean-Louis, *October 23*
Fortuny y Marsal, Mariano, *June 11*
Foujita, Tsugouharu, *November 27*
Fragonard, Jean Honoré, *April 4*

Francis, Sam, *June 25*
Frankenthaler, Helen, *December 12*
Freud, Lucian, *December 8*
Friedrich, Caspar David, *September 5*
Friesz, Othon, *February 6*
Frith, William Powell, *January 9*
Fromentin, Eugène, *October 24*
Furness, Frank, *November 12*
Fuseli, Henry, *February 6*

G

Gabo, Naum, *August 5*
Gainsborough, Thomas, *May 14*
Gallé, Émile, *May 4*
Garnier, Charles, *November 6*
Gaudí, Antoni, *June 25*
Gauguin, Paul, *June 7*
Gavarni, Paul, *January 13*
Gehry, Frank, *February 28*
Géricault, Théodore, *September 26*
Giacometti, Alberto, *October 10*
Gibbons, Grinling, *April 4*
Gibson, Charles Dana, *September 14*
Gilbert, Cass, *November 24*
Gilbert, Sir John, *July 21*
Gillray, James, *August 13*
Giordano, Luca, *October 18*

Givenchy, Hubert de, *February 21*
Glackens, William, *March 13*
Gleizes, Albert, *December 8*
Goddard, John, *January 20*
Gogh, Vincent van, *March 30*
Goldin, Nan, *September 12*
Goldsworthy, Andy, *July 26*
Gontcharova, Natalia, *June 16*
Gonzáles, Julio, *September 21*
Gorky, Arshile, *April 15*
Gornik, April, *April 20*
Goya, Francisco de, *March 30*
Goyen, Jan Josephsz. van, *January 13*
Grandville, Jean Jacques, *September 15*
Granet, François-Marius, *December 17*
Gravelot, Hubert-François, *March 26*
Graves, Morris, *August 28*
Graves, Nancy, *December 23*
Gray, Eileen, *August 9*
Greenaway, Kate, *March 17*
Greenough, Horatio, *September 6*
Greuze, Jean Baptiste, *August 21*
Gris, Juan, *March 23*
Grooms, Red, *June 1*
Gropius, Walter, *May 18*
Gros, Baron Antoine-Jean, *March 16*
Grossman, Nancy, *April 28*
Grosz, George, *July 26*
Guardi, Francesco, *October 5*
Guercino, *February 2*

Guidi, Domenico, *June 6*
Guillaumin, Armand, *February 16*
Günther, Ignaz, *November 22*
Gursky, Andreas, *January 15*
Guston, Philip, *June 27*
Guy, Seymour Joseph, *January 16*
Gwathmey, Charles, *June 19*

H

Halston, *April 23*
Hamilton, Ann, *June 22*
Hardenbergh, Henry, *February 6*
Harnett, William M., *August 10*
Harrison, Peter, *June 14*
Hartigan, Grace, *March 28*
Hartley, Marsden, *January 4*
Hartung, Hans, *September 21*
Hassam, Childe, *October 17*
Heade, Martin Johnson, *August 11*
Heckel, Erich, *July 31*
Held, Al, *October 12*
Held, John, Jr., *January 10*
Hélion, Jean, *April 21*
Helleu, Paul César, *December 17*
Henneberg, Hugo, *July 27*
Henri, Robert, *June 24*
Hepworth, Barbara, *January 10*

Herter, Albert, *March 2*
Hildebrand, Adolf von, *October 6*
Hildebrandt, Johann Lukas von, *November 14*
Hine, Lewis W., *September 26*
Hirst, Damien, *June 7*
Hoadley, David, *April 29*
Hobbema, Meindert, *October 31*
Hockney, David, *July 9*
Hodgkin, Howard, *August 6*
Hoffman, Malvina, *June 15*
Hofmann, Hans, *March 21*
Hogarth, William, *November 10*
Hokusai, Katsushika, *October 21*
Holabird, William, *September 11*
Hollar, Wenceslaus, *July 23*
Homer, Winslow, *February 24*
Hooch, Pieter de, *December 20*
Hopper, Edward, *July 22*
Houdon, Jean-Antoine, *March 25*
Hovenden, Thomas, *December 28*
Howard, Charles, *January 2*
Hume, Gary, *May 9*
Hunt, Richard Morris, *October 31*
Hunt, William Holman, *April 2*
Hunt, William Morris, *March 31*

I

Indiana, Robert, *September 13*
Ingres, J. A. D., *August 29*
Inness, George, *May 1*
Ipoustéguy, Jean, *January 6*
Ives, James Merritt, *March 5*

J

James, Charles, *July 18*
Jawlensky, Alexej von, *March 26*
Jefferson, Thomas, *April 13*
Jensen, Georg, *August 31*
Johns, Jasper, *May 15*
Johnson, Eastman, *July 29*
Johnson, Philip, *July 8*
Johnston, Frances B., *January 15*
Jones, Inigo, *July 19*
Jongkind, Johan Barthold, *June 3*
Jordaens, Jacob, *May 20*
Judd, Donald, *June 3*
Juhl, Finn, *January 30*
Juvarra, Filippo, *June 16*

K

Kahn, Louis I., *February 20*
Kandinsky, Wassily, *December 4*
Kapoor, Anish, *March 12*
Katz, Alex, *July 24*
Kauffman, Angelica, *October 30*
Kelly, Ellsworth, *May 31*
Kendrick, Mel, *July 28*
Kensett, John Frederick, *March 22*
Kent, Rockwell, *June 21*
Kentridge, William, *April 28*
Kertész, André, *July 2*
Kiefer, Anselm, *March 8*
Kirchner, Ernst Ludwig, *May 6*
Kitaj, R. B., *October 29*
Klee, Paul, *December 18*
Klein, William, *April 19*
Klein, Yves, *April 28*
Klimt, Gustav, *July 14*
Kline, Franz, *May 23*
Klinger, Max, *February 18*
Kneller, Sir Godfrey, *August 8*
Kokoschka, Oskar, *March 1*
Kollwitz, Käthe, *July 8*
Koninck, Philips, *November 5*
Koons, Jeff, *January 21*
Krasner, Lee, *October 27*
Kühn, Heinrich, *February 25*
Kuhn, Walt, *October 27*
Kuitca, Guillermo, *January 22*
Kuniyoshi, Yasuo, *September 1*
Kupka, František, *September 22*

L

L'Enfant, Pierre Charles, *August 2*
La Farge, John, *March 31*
La Fresnaye, Robert de, *July 11*
La Tour, Georges de, *March 14*
La Tour, Maurice-Quentin de, *September 5*
Lachaise, Gaston, *May 19*
Lafever, Minard, *August 10*
Lalique, René, *April 6*
Lancret, Nicolas, *January 22*
Landseer, Sir Edwin, *March 7*
Landseer Lutyens, Sir Edwin, *March 29*
Lane, Fitz Hugh, *December 19*
Lanfranco, Giovanni, *January 26*
Lange, Dorothea, *May 26*
Lannuier, Charles-Honoré, *June 27*
Larsson, Carl, *May 28*
Laurent, Robert, *June 29*
Lawrence, Jacob, *September 7*
Lawrence, Sir Thomas, *April 13*
Le Brun, Charles, *February 24*
Le Prince, Jean-Baptiste, *September 17*
Le Sueur, Eustache, *November 19*
Leach, Bernard, *January 5*
Lear, Edward, *May 12*
Ledoux, Claude-Nicolas, *March 21*
Leech, John, *August 29*
Léger, Fernand, *February 4*
Legros, Alphonse, *May 8*
Legros, Pierre, *May 27*
Lehmbruck, Wilhelm, *January 4*
Leibl, Wilhelm, *October 23*
Lely, Sir Peter, *September 14*
Lemoyne, Jean-Baptiste, *February 19*
Leonardo da Vinci, *April 15*
Leutze, Emanuel, *May 24*
Levine, Jack, *January 3*
Leyendecker, Joseph Christian, *March 23*
Lichtenstein, Roy, *October 28*
Liebermann, Max, *July 20*
Lipchitz, Jacques, *August 22*
Lippold, Richard, *May 3*
Lissitzky, El, *November 23*
Loos, Adolph, *December 10*
Lorrain, Robert Le, *November 15*
Louis, Morris, *November 28*
Luks, George, *August 13*
Lurçat, Jean, *July 1*

M

Macke, August, *January 3*

Mackintosh, Charles Rennie, *June 7*
MacMonnies, Frederick William, *September 28*
Magritte, René, *November 21*
Maillol, Aristide, *October 8*
Mainbocher, *October 24*
Malevich, Kazimir, *February 26*
Man Ray, *August 25*
Manet, Édouard, *January 23*
Mansart, François, *January 23*
Mansart, Jules Hardouin, *April 16*
Manship, Paul, *December 25*
Manzù, Giacomo, *December 22*
Mapplethorpe, Robert, *November 4*
Maratti, Carlo, *May 18*
Marc, Franz, *February 8*
Marin, John, *December 23*
Marini, Marino, *February 27*
Maris, Jacob, *August 25*
Marisol, *May 22*
Marsh, Reginald, *March 14*
Martin, John, *July 19*
Masaccio, *December 21*
Matisse, Henri, *December 31*
McIntire, Samuel, *January 16*
McKim, Charles, *August 24*
Meidner, Ludwig, *April 18*
Mendelsohn, Eric, *March 21*
Mengs, Anton Raphael, *March 12*
Michelangelo Buonarroti, *March 6*
Mies van der Rohe, Ludwig, *March 27*

Millais, Sir John Everett, *June 8*
Miller, Kenneth Hayes, *March 11*
Milles, Carl, *June 23*
Millet, Jean François, *October 4*
Mills, Clark, *December 13*
Miró, Joan, *April 20*
Mochi, Francesco, *July 29*
Modigliani, Amedeo, *July 12*
Moholy-Nagy, Lázló, *July 20*
Mollino, Carlo, *May 6*
Mondrian, Piet, *March 7*
Monet, Claude, *November 14*
Monnot, Pierre-Etienne, *August 9*
Montañés, Juan Martínez, *March 16*
Moore, Henry, *July 30*
Moran, Thomas, *February 12*
Morandi, Giorgio, *July 20*
Moreau, Gustave, *April 6*
Morisot, Berthe, *January 14*
Morland, George, *June 26*
Morris, Robert, *February 9*
Morris, William, *March 24*
Morse, Samuel F. B., *April 27*
Moser, Koloman, *March 30*
Moses, Grandma, *September 7*
Motherwell, Robert, *January 24*
Mount, William Sidney, *November 26*
Mucha, Alphonse, *July 24*
Munch, Edvard, *December 12*
Murillo, Bartolomé Esteban, *January 1*

Muybridge, Eadweard, *April 9*

N

Nadar, *April 8*
Nadelman, Elie, *February 20*
Nakian, Reuben, *August 10*
Nast, Thomas, *September 27*
Nelson, George, *May 29*
Neshat, Shirin, *March 26*
Neumann, Balthasar, *January 30*
Neutra, Richard, *April 8*
Newman, Arnold, *March 3*
Newman, Barnett, *January 29*
Nicholson, Ben, *April 10*
Niemeyer, Oscar, *December 15*
Noguchi, Isamu, *November 17*
Nolan, Sidney, *April 22*
Noland, Kenneth, *April 10*
Nolde, Emil, *August 7*

O

O'Keeffe, Georgia, *November 15*
Ofili, Chris, *October 10*
Oldenburg, Claes, *January 28*

Olmsted, Frederick Law, *April 26*
Oppenord, Gilles-Marie, *July 27*
Orozco, José, *November 23*
Ostade, Adriaen van, *December 10*
Oud, J. J. P., *February 9*
Oudry, Jean-Baptiste, *March 17*
Oursler, Tony, *May 19*

P

Palladio, Andrea, *November 8*
Palmer, Samuel, *January 27*
Parmigianino, *January 11*
Parrish, Maxfield, *July 25*
Pater, Jean Baptiste, *December 29*
Paxton, Joseph, *August 3*
Peale, Charles Willson, *April 15*
Peale, Raphaelle, *February 17*
Peale, Rembrandt, *February 22*
Pechstein, Max, *December 31*
Penn, Irving, *June 16*
Pennell, Joseph, *July 4*
Percier, Charles, *August 22*
Pereira, I. Rice, *August 5*
Pevsner, Antoine, *January 18*
Piazzetta, Giovanni Battista, *February 13*
Picabia, Francis, *January 22*
Picasso, Pablo, *October 25*

Pigalle, Jean-Baptiste, *January 26*
Pinelli, Bartolomeo, *November 20*
Pippin, Horace, *February 22*
Piranesi, Giovanni Battista, *October 4*
Pissarro, Camille, *July 10*
Pollock, Jackson, *January 28*
Pompon, François, *May 9*
Pontormo, Jacopo da, *May 26*
Poons, Larry, *October 1*
Pope, John Russell, *April 24*
Porter, Eliot, *December 6*
Porter, Fairfield, *June 10*
Potter, Beatrix, *July 28*
Potter, Paulus, *November 20*
Powers, Hiram, *July 29*
Pradier, Jean, *May 23*
Pratt, Matthew, *September 23*
Preti, Mattia, *February 24*
Prout, Samuel, *September 17*
Prud'hon, Pierre-Paul, *April 4*
Puget, Pierre, *October 16*
Pugin, A. W. N., *March 1*
Pyle, Howard, *March 5*

R

Rackham, Arthur, *September 19*
Raeburn, Sir Henry, *March 4*

Raphael, *April 6*
Rauschenberg, Robert, *October 22*
Redon, Odilon, *April 20*
Regnault, Jean-Baptiste, *October 17*
Reid, John Robertson, *August 6*
Reinhardt, Ad, *December 24*
Rembrandt, *July 15*
Remington, Frederic, *October 4*
Reni, Guido, *November 4*
Renoir, Pierre-Auguste, *February 25*
Repton, Humphry, *April 21*
Revere, Paul, *January 1*
Reynolds, Sir Joshua, *July 16*
Ribalta, Francisco, *June 2*
Ribera, Jusepe de, *February 17*
Richardson, Henry Hobson, *September 29*
Richter, Gerhard, *February 9*
Rigaud, Hyacinthe, *July 18*
Riis, Jacob, *May 3*
Ringgold, Faith, *October 8*
Rivera, Diego, *December 13*
Rivers, Larry, *August 17*
Robbia, Andrea della, *October 20*
Robert, Hubert, *May 22*
Roche, Kevin, *June 14*
Rockwell, Norman, *February 3*
Rodin, Auguste, *November 12*
Roebling, John, *June 12*
Romney, George, *December 26*
Root, John Wellborn, *January 10*

Rops, Félicien, *July 7*
Rosenquist, James, *November 29*
Rossetti, Dante Gabriel, *May 12*
Rothko, Mark, *September 25*
Rouault, Georges, *May 27*
Rousseau, Henri, *May 21*
Rubens, Peter Paul, *June 28*
Rude, François, *January 4*
Runge, Philipp Otto, *July 23*
Ruscha, Edward, *December 16*
Rusconi, Camillo, *July 14*
Rush, William, *July 4*
Ruskin, John, *February 8*
Ryder, Albert Pinkham, *March 19*
Rysbrack, Michael, *June 27*

S

Saar, Alison, *February 5*
Saarinen, Eero, *August 20*
Saarinen, Eliel, *August 20*
Saenredam, Pieter, *June 9*
Saint Laurent, Yves, *August 1*
Saint-Aubin, Augustin de, *January 3*
Saint-Aubin, Gabriel de, *April 14*
Saint-Gaudens, Augustus, *March 1*
Salle, David, *September 28*
Sargent, John Singer, *January 12*

Sassoferrato, *August 25*
Sax, Adolphe, *November 6*
Scarpa, Carlo, *June 2*
Schindler, Rudolph, *September 5*
Schinkel, Karl Fredrich, *March 13*
Schlemmer, Oskar, *September 4*
Schnabel, Julian, *October 26*
Schwitters, Kurt, *June 20*
Scorel, Jan van, *August 1*
Scully, Sean, *June 30*
Segal, George, *November 26*
Senefelder, J. N. F. Alois, *November 6*
Sequeira, Domingos de, *March 10*
Séraphine, Louis, *September 2*
Serlio, Sebastiano, *September 6*
Serra, Richard, *November 2*
Seurat, Georges-Pierre, *December 2*
Severini, Gino, *April 7*
Shahn, Ben, *September 12*
Shannon, J. J., *February 3*
Sharp, William, *January 29*
Shaw, Richard Norman, *May 7*
Sheeler, Charles, *July 16*
Sherman, Cindy, *January 19*
Sickert, Walter, *May 31*
Signac, Paul, *November 11*
Simmons, Laurie, *October 3*
Simpson, Lorna, *August 13*
Singh, Raghubir, *October 22*
Sisley, Alfred, *October 30*

Sloan, John, *August 2*
Slodtz, René-Michel, *September 27*
Smibert, John, *March 24*
Smith, David, *March 9*
Smith, Kiki, *January 18*
Smith, W. Eugene, *December 30*
Smithson, Robert, *January 2*
Snyders, Frans, *November 11*
Soane, Sir John, *September 10*
Soleri, Paolo, *June 21*
Sorolla y Bastida, Joaquín, *February 27*
Soufflot, Jacques-Germain, *July 23*
Soyer, Raphael, *December 25*
Staël, Nicolas de, *January 5*
Starck, Philippe, *January 18*
Steichen, Edward, *March 27*
Steinberg, Saul, *June 15*
Steinway, Henry, *February 15*
Stella, Joseph, *June 13*
Stevens, Alfred, *May 11*
Stiegel, Henry William, *May 13*
Stieglitz, Alfred, *January 1*
Strand, Paul, *October 16*
Stuart, Gilbert, *December 3*
Sullivan, Louis, *September 3*
Sully, Thomas, *June 19*
Sultan, Donald, *May 5*
Sutcliffe, Frank M., *October 6*

White, Stanford, *November 9*
Wilkie, Sir David, *November 18*
Wilson, Richard, *August 1*
Winters, Terry, *June 1*
Wood, Grant, *February 13*
Wren, Sir Christopher, *October 20*
Wright, Frank Lloyd, *June 8*
Wright, Russel, *April 3*
Wyatt, James, *August 3*
Wyeth, Andrew, *July 12*

Y

Youngerman, Jack, *March 25*

Z

Zadkine, Ossip, *July 14*
Zoffany, Johann, *March 13*
Zuccarelli, Francesco, *August 15*
Zurbarán, Francisco de, *November 7*